Contents

KT-440-361

Eureka moment!

Learn about important discoveries that have brought about further knowledge and understanding.

DID YOU KNOW?

Discover fascinating facts about electricity.

WHAT'S NEXT?

Read about the latest research and advances in essential physical science.

Some words are shown in bold, **like this**. You can find out what they mean by looking in the glossary.

What is electricity?

Electricity is a form of **energy** that we use to power most of the machines we use every day. It is the flow of electrical power from tiny parts called **atoms**. Everything in the world is made up of atoms, which are so small we cannot see them. Even the tiniest things have an enormous number of atoms. For example, a grain of salt has around 10,000 trillion atoms!

An atom is made of three types of parts: **protons** and **neutrons** at its centre, and **electrons** that travel round and round them very quickly. Electricity occurs when electrons flow from atom to atom.

Then and now

Before people discovered how to make electricity, they kept warm by burning wood or coal in fireplaces. They used candles and oil lamps to light their homes, and ice to keep food cold. Today we use electricity to power lights, fridge-freezers, televisions, computers, and many other machines. We take electricity for granted – but life would be very different without it!

Electric lights and instruments help to make live rock shows loud, colourful, and exciting for massive audiences.